Murray The Milkman

Flowers & Seeds

By

Stephen Molokwu

One sunny morning Murray's milk-mobile parked up at Farmer Gribbles' farm. Murray jumped out.

"Hey Farmer Gribbles!" Murray shouted.

Farmer Gribbles appeared. "Hello there Murray me old mucker," said Farmer Gribbles. They did the milkman handshake.

"Now what can I do for you today then Murray?" Farmer Gribbles asked as he picked his nose.

"Well," Murray replied, "Miss Twitch asked me to pick up some daffodil seeds, blue-bell seeds and some marigold seeds for the children to plant."

Farmer Gribbles looked puzzled. "Ah yes I remember now," he said and pulled out three bags from his pocket.

"A very nice choice of flowers indeed," said Farmer Gribbles. "As Mrs Gribbles always says 'happy flowers make happy people.'"

Murray smiled and got back into the milk-mobile. "Thanks Farmer Gribbles."

Farmer Gribbles waved goodbye. "You take care now Murray," he chuckled as Murray drove off.

The milk-mobile arrived at the school. Miss Twitch was planting baby trees with some children.

Murray climbed out of the milk-mobile. "Hello Miss Twitch," he said.

Miss Twitch smiled, "Murray, just the man I wanted to see."

Murray gave her the seeds.

"Thank you very much," said Miss Twitch.

Suddenly Dionne and Daniel came running up to them. "Hello Uncle Murray!" they shouted.

"Hey kids, what are you two up to then?" Murray asked.

Daniel was out of breath. "We've been helping Miss Twitch plant trees," he replied. "Trees and flowers grow from seeds."

"Miss Twitch said it's important to plant trees because they help us breathe by making oxygen," added Dionne.

Murray smiled, "Miss Twitch is a very good teacher," he said.

"Well I did win teacher of the year three times in a row!" laughed Miss Twitch.

"What kind of trees are you planting today Miss Twitch?" He asked.

"Well," said Miss Twitch. "This morning we've planted Sycamore Trees, the ones with seeds that fall like helicopters."

Daniel pulled out an acorn from his pocket. "And we planted Oak Trees. They have acorns!" He exclaimed.

"That's right," said Miss Twitch. "Oak trees grow big and strong, and are used to make a lot of furniture."

"Do you know what furniture is kids?" asked Murray.

Daniel put his hand up, "I know, I know," he cried. "Is it like tables and chairs made from wood?"

"That's right," said Murray.

Dionne pulled a face at Daniel. "Clever clogs," she said. Daniel pulled a face back at Dionne.

"Now, now children," said Miss Twitch.

"What flowers will the seeds grow into Miss Twitch?" asked Murray.

Miss Twitch smiled and said, "Well, if you come with me, I'll show you." With that, they all walked into the school.

As they walked off, Rascal showed up in the distance and hid behind a hedge.

"This time the milk will be mine, hee hee!" said Rascal.

Rascal tip-toed up to the milk-mobile. "This time I can't fail. The milk will be mine, hee hee!" he cried.

Rascal grabbed as many bottles of milk as his little arms could carry and ran off. "I've got the milk!" said Rascal.

Elsewhere, inside the school gardens Miss Twitch, and Dionne and Daniel were showing Murray the flowers that had already grown.

"We planted these a few weeks ago Uncle Murray," said Dionne. She pointed to some flowers with yellow leaves. "These are called Daffodils," she said.

Then, Daniel pointed to some flowers with blue leaves in the shape of a small bell. "Uncle Murray, these are called Blue Bells. They really do look like blue bells." Daniel said.

"Yes they do," smiled Murray. "They're almost as beautiful as Miss Twitch."

"But not quite!" She laughed.

Next Murray pointed to some flowers with bright orange petals. "What are these called?" He asked.

"They're called Marigolds," replied Dionne.

Murray smelled the flowers. "I think I might have to get some of these for my garden," he said. "I better cut the weeds first though."

Everyone laughed.

Elsewhere, there was a bush with moving vines. As Rascal appeared, the vines stopped moving.

Rascal made sure there was no one around before he sat down in front of the bush. "Finally some tasty milk!" he said.

Rascal lifted the milk to his lips and was about to take a huge gulp, when suddenly the vines from the bush reached down and scooped up his milk!

"No! No!" Rascal shouted. He jumped up and down trying to get the milk but his little arms were too short to reach it.

He jumped up and down until he was too tired to jump anymore. Finally, Rascal sat down and began to cry.

"Waaaa," he cried. "The bush won't give me my milk. Boo hoo waaaaa."

THE END